I0440548

The Bankers Rules
Financial Secrets

Family Financial Lessons:
How compound interest will keep you wealthy.

Copyright 2024

Interact with me on YouTube
Youtube.com/@bankersrules

Author Jeff Steinbrunner

Family Dynasty Financial Lessons:
Growing Wealth Together
Generational Wealth Blueprint

In financial education, the concept of a Family Dynasty revolves around cultivating wealth collaboratively across generations. This approach emphasizes a Generational Wealth Blueprint, highlighting the importance of passing down financial knowledge, strategies, and values from one family member to the next.

By actively involving family members in the process of wealth creation and management, individuals aim to establish a lasting legacy that transcends time.

The focus extends beyond immediate financial gains, encompassing a holistic perspective that considers both short-term goals and long-term sustainability. Through shared experiences and a commitment to financial literacy, families aspire to build a strong financial foundation that can withstand the test of time and positively impact future generations.

DISCLAIMER

The content provided in this book is designed to provide helpful information on the subjects discussed.

The numbers in this book are theoretical and are to be used for illustrative purposes only. The publisher and the author are not responsible for any actions you take or do not take as a result of reading this book and are not liable for any damages or negative consequences from action to any person reading or following the information in this book.

References are provided for informational purposes only and do not constitute endorsement of any websites or other sources. Readers should also be aware that the websites listed in this book may change or become obsolete.

Table of contents

From the Author,

I have written this book to see if what I have done to build wealth on basically autopilot will work for you. My hope is that you will be able to replicate the lessons in this book and get the same or better results than me.

May you grow wealthier and wiser..... Here's to your success!

Introduction

In this book you will learn how compound interest builds wealth. The power of interest compounding in your favor day after day. Interest working for you in a private credit line you control. If you follow the rules in this book you will be one of the few people that grow their money on the right side of interest.

But to get started on this journey you will need some money set aside for your very own line of credit. The line of credit is for your very own private bank. This concept bank needs some money to make you loans. The money won't just appear, it has to come from somewhere. It can be gifted to you but it will most likely not just appear. The amount can be as little as $20 to $2000, the point is that you need some money to start with. If you haven't any extra money you can start saving while you learn these rules of being your own private bank.

Greatest Banking Dynasty Ever

The Rothschild's the greatest banking Dynasty that ever lived. Still around today, still the wealthiest family. You will learn some of their secrets to build your banking dynasty, your riches just like the Rothschild's.

   The Rothschild's started out in the slums of Germany. Mayer Rothschild was not as wealthy as the Vanderbilt or Rockefeller yet today is the greatest Dynasty in the history of the world. Mayor Rothschild and his five sons span the globe running central banks all over the world.
   Now you can learn to implement the banker's rules that were created and used by Mayor Rothschild.

   You may not have noticed all the banks are owned by individuals or families. This is a clue that anyone can do this. But I'm not talking about getting a banking charter or buying a building. I'm talking about using the same rules that make the banker rich.

Lesson 1.
The Banking concept

In this book, we are not talking about getting a charter or a banking license. You will learn how to structure a vehicle (that is where you put your money) for lending to yourself. WARNING!!! (I don't recommend lending to others without knowing the lending laws in your area.) The bank that you'll be setting up is not a physical bank. This Bank is a concept bank. The purpose of this bank is to build wealth by redirecting the money leaving your pocket and redirecting it back into your pocket, with interest.

If you're like I was and the majority of people, you are unaware that around 40% of the money you earn goes right back out to interest, taxes, and other entities. The purpose of this book is to help you redirect some of the 40% back to you, instead of other institutions.

If you follow these rules and principles, I believe you'll become wealthier and keep more of your money than you ever thought imaginable.

To start you need to fund your bank. The money won't just appear out of thin air. As I said before in the interdiction. You probably might be thinking, where am I going to come up with the funds for this?
Well, that answer is simple, any money that you have put back can be used to start funding your bank. A line of credit or money you saved in a penny jar.

As an example; I had $400 set aside. I then borrowed $400 from my personal bank to repair my driveway. I paid back the $400 plus 20% interest back to my personal bank, equaling $500.
The key is to pay yourself back plus the interest. I hope you understand the simplicity and greatness this principle is! Over time, you can build a great future. But more on that later.
This is the same concept as starting a business and putting aside money for the business. In both cases, you need to have money separate from your personal money.

So think of it like this, it's your bank's money, not yours. You may control the bank but keep it separate from your personal household and/ or business finances.

You can keep it in a vehicle like a hi-yield savings account, or a money market account so that you can make more interest until you're ready to lend out the money.

Lesson 2.
Funding your Bank

Lets go more in-depth and explain how to go about funding your bank. There are many different ways to fund your bank. Here are a few examples you can use.

- You may fund your bank from your own checking account.
- You may fund your bank from money you have in a tin can.
- You may fund your bank through a life insurance policy.
- You may fund your bank through a line of credit.
- You may use a hi-yield savings account,or a money market account.

There are many different ways that you may fund your bank. There are many ideas in many ways you can draw in money.
So, to fund your bank, you just need to choose one or even use them all. There is no wrong way. However, you must make sure that you have sufficient funds. You can not overdraw your bank. You must be diligent to track all expenses and deposits. For if you don't do so you will run out of money and maybe in financial trouble if you borrowed any money. There are many apps to help track your experience or you can do it old-school on paper. You can use income and expense sheets and or assets and liability sheets. But you must track every cent! *See bonus page 26 in this book.*

For example, *see picture.*

≡ B1 Bank Cash Flow	🔍	📅	⋮

Balance:	$7,960.25
Verified:	$7,960.25

✅	**My Credit** Payment Nov 03, 2023	$554.00 $7,960.25
✅	**Kettering** Paycheck Nov 02, 2023	$3,702.40 $7,406.25
✅	**Homedepot** Sale Of Goods Oct 30, 2023	$253.63 $3,703.85
✅	**Living Expenses** Loan Oct 27, 2023	$1,325.00 $3,957.48
✅	**Kettering** Paycheck Oct 05, 2023	$1,282.48 $5,282.48

Lesson 3.
Mindset *(the banks money)*

Rule 1. Be disciplined, manage your money.

Have control over your spending habits. The power you get as a banker is the same power you can abuse. As a banker, you have access to money that you can be tempted to spend.

You may want items like a new car or new clothes. Remember if you're using your private bank to buy things. You must pay back your bank plus interest at least the same as any other lender. Say around 6%to 20% for example. I'm not suggesting you should not buy things but remember the bank should not buy them for you. You need to pay back the money with interest to your bank.

Rule 2. Pay back your bank plus interest.

When you lend money to yourself to buy something, pay it back exactly the same way and at the same percentage rate just as if you borrowed it from another lender. You can set the rate to charge. Like 3%-20%. If you miss a payment make sure to pay the late charges back to your bank. Say $30 late fee. Pay that late payment as soon as possible! This rule bankers tend to break because they have the power not to pay themselves. This is the first step to the demise of your bank. This rule cannot be overstated. You will learn about how to structure your underwriting in lesson 4.

Rule 3. Think of your bank as a separate entity.

When you borrow money from your bank, treat it as you would any other lender or Bank. The biggest challenge is keeping this mindset. It is easy for some people but harder for others. Being a successful Banker, is getting rid of the human problem. Do not spend every cent you have. You need a different mindset. You need to think like a banker. That is why the bankers' rules are so important. You must overcome your spending habits, turn them into saving habits with interest. You can and must adopt the bankers' habits.

Building wealth through interest is like creating money. Think of it, when a bank charges interest on a loan that money does not exist. The original amount say, one hundred dollars but the interest does not. Now the money won't just appear. Someone aka the *borrower* has to work to pay the difference. That is one way banks build such massive wealth, and now that you know you can also. "It's good to be the banker!"

Lesson 4.
Structure and underwriting

Structure = how much you can lend, late fees, amount per transaction %, etc.
Underwriting= the Guidelines on how you lend. What you will and what you won't lend money for.
Example
Lending amount
$30,000 total
No more than $4,000 on credit line @ 20% interest.
No more than $10,000 on each secured loan @ 6% interest like a car.
Late fees $30.
No unsecured loan exception on my credit line.
 These are the guidelines you set for your bank to keep you in line. This should help you to keep out the human desires, that of want over building the wealth mindset. Think of your bank as a separate entity like an LLC. You don't need to put the bank in a legal entity, but you should treat it like you don't own it. Though you do. On the other hand, you need

to run the bank as a financial business. Your bank is in business to make money. As a fictional example, (using the word I instead of Jim or Michael.) I built my bank over time by buying the loans I owed. I took over my car payment, then I bought a camper and bought out that loan and then bought the mortgage on my house. All in 3 years time. My private bank paid about $98,000.00 to buy those assets. Today I owe my bank over $260,000.00. That includes the principle plus the interest. I paid off all my lender's, and those loans became my bank's assets. If I sold all my assets today, I would have around $140,000.00, the rest is unsecured loan debt, I owe $120,000.00 to my credit line. No, I'm not a millionaire but not bad for just 3 years.

How much can you lend

How much you can lend depends on how much money your bank has. Be disciplined! Unless you are buying up a loan you have with another lender or need to get work done on your vehicle. Make small loans. Make sure you keep your private bank's money separate from your personal money. Never mix the two. Try to keep the debt you create within your means. After all, you have to pay back your bank principal plus the interest.

Over time your money will keep growing as long as you pay your loans. If done correctly you can buy assets like apartment buildings that pay you to own them. You can lend money to start a business that can help get you free from working a 9-5 if you want. You can even keep working the job you're at if you have no desire to leave.

Charging late fees

Yes, you should charge late fees. If you borrowed the money from a bank you better believe they would not think twice about changing you. I myself don't like to pay late fees. But as a banker, on the other hand I love making money. In your underwriting set as example a $30.00 late fee.

Balance:	-$249,230.00
Verified:	-$249,230.00

Late Fee — $30.00
Missed Payment
Nov 11, 2023 — -$249,230.00

House — $700.00
Mortgage
Sep 05, 2023 — -$249,200.00

House — $700.00
Mortgage
Aug 22, 2023 — -$249,900.00

Set amount per transaction %

Decide your percentage rate. The rate that you will charge. 3%,6%,12%, you get the idea. I chose 20% because I didn't like to spend my money. This gets me to think, do I really want or need to buy something. You can charge the percentage rate that is right for you or after paying off something like a car say 2 years early just start paying the rest of the payments back to your bank as if you still have that loan. For example: if you paid $300.00 per month, then you keep paying that same $300.00 to your private bank. For that 2 year term. Make sure you keep track of your payments so you know when it's paid off.

Structuring your Underwriting

Underwriting is your lending guidelines on how you will lend. That's right you decide how your money gets lent out. Do you lend with or without collateral? Will you lend on income producing real estate? Sense most people won't be lending to others at first let me give an example:

You need to minimize the risk of every loan by setting a credit limit. Let's set the limit. If you have $10,000 to lend. Let's say you make $40,000.00 net after taxes. If you're *liabilities,* that is your household bills, food, gas etc is $30,000.00. Make your line of credit $2,000 to $3,000 this gives you the ability to make other loans. Let's make it a $3,000 line of credit. Think of this as a credit card. You make this a debit in your bank ledger. You decide to lend this $3,000 at 6%. You can use it for an emergency fund or just to make a 6% on your daily purchase.

Now this Leaves $7,000 to make other loans. In this example let's pay off a car loan you have with another lender. Say the payoff is $4,256.62. You pay off that lender 2 years early. Leaving you $2,743.38 in your wealth account. Plus what is in your line of credit. Now in your private bank you make a new loan entry as a debit of $5,640. This is the remaining balance of the car loan. Now if your payments were $235 a month keeping the payment the same. In that way it's like nothing changed. Except you now have an asset paying you $235 a month totaling $5,640 over the loan term. An extra $5,640 coming back into your wealth account. Instead of that other lender receiving your money. Or you can refinance it with a new 5 year loan. Which will make your bank $14,100 excluding the original payoff. Still just paying $235 a month but over 60 months.

Are you seeing how you will build your wealth and keep it? I bet you wish you knew this secret sooner. A secret that has been hidden in plain sight.

Lesson 5.

Refinance your loans through your bank

You may have heard of The Snowball Effect. That's where you pay off a bill and take the money and put that towards another bill, and continue doing this until you paid off all your bills.
One thing that might work better. I'd like to call, *the avalanche effect*. This is where you pay off one bill, take that money, and pay it back to your private bank, your own line of credit. Just as you would have kept paying to your other creditor.
(like the example in the last lesson). This method puts the wealth back into your pocket. As you build up that wealth as you make each monthly payment back to your bank, you will start to see how the compounding of interest will work in your favor. Once you have the money to cover another lender. Then you can take out a loan from your wealth account, aka your private bank. Payoff that lender, and now you have taken over that loan. Now you have 2 loans that you will be paying into your private bank. Plus don't forget about your line of credit. This gives you velocity of money. Now, you have two loans and a credit line compounding interest into your credit line.

Your own private bank. This is the secret of how compound interest will keep you wealthy. You may think that because you spent the money on that other loan that your first amount is gone. Depending on how you do this, it may take some time to get the compounding interest to be noticeable. Keep at it, and as your bank builds more wealth so you will too.

By refinancing your loan through your private bank, you redirect the money that was flowing out of your pocket back into your pocket with interest. Creating new loans instead of just buying them up, gives you higher returns. Helping you to build up more money for your future. Keep in mind that on assets like a car loan, the collateral is losing value. Most people also buy a new vehicle every 3 to 5 years. So if the vehicle is still in good condition and you think that you'll keep it for a long time, refinance. Otherwise just repay the rest of the original loan.

Assets like apartment buildings, single family housing usually goes up in value. Normally over time.

Building equity in the property allows you to leverage your assets to build wealth faster than using your own bank.

More on that in the next lesson.

Lesson 6.
Build a legacy (*family bank*)

If you're interested in lending money to your children or other family members, consider using your established family bank. Your family bank is your family-owned, family-funded entity, designated to build wealth, structured correctly such as a family limited partnership or dynasty trust. It is designed with one purpose in mind, making intra-family loans. Also allows you to build generational wealth. You may make loans for vehicles, student loans, business loans etc. As an example:
 An intra-family loan lets a borrower finance a home with funds lent by a relative. It can save the borrower money and helps build your family's wealth. It also acts as an estate-planning tool for the lender.
An intra-family housing loan is not, and cannot be, a casual arrangement. It must be a formal loan, set up carefully to avoid being foolish about the tax laws. Both borrower and lender must stick to a repayment schedule, including applicable interest charges, to avoid having the loan construed as a gift, which can have major tax implications.

Just a suggestion, your bank can buy the real estate and land contract the property to your other family members.This may get you around getting a lending license in some states.

Warning
There are significant legal and tax considerations around intra-family housing loans, it's highly advisable to consult an attorney or tax expert familiar with these matters to help ensure your loan is structured and documented in a way that will withstand IRS scrutiny, and that both parties involved in the loan report payment and interest information correctly on their federal tax returns.

The components of an Intra-family Loan

The following component must be part of an intra-family loan to be considered a loan and not a gift from family members by the IRS.

Set your Loan Terms

For an intra-family housing loan to be legitimate in the eyes of the IRS, it must be a formal loan with a fixed installment payment amount and a set repayment schedule. And in nearly all cases of intrafamily housing loans, interest rates must be charged.

While regular payments are essential, they need not follow the monthly payment schedule common to most traditional mortgages. If the borrower and lender prefer, payments may be due quarterly or even annually. This arrangement often works well when the housing loan is used for a fix and flip or to transfer property for estate-planning purposes.

The family member(s) issuing the loan will need to report interest they receive on the loan as income when submitting annual income returns. The recipient of the loan may deduct interest charges on the loan from their federal income tax return if they itemize their deductions.

Why use Intra-family Loans
If you're fortunate enough to have the means to provide a home loan for your children or grandchildren, it's worth considering an intra-family loan under any of the following circumstances:
Interest rates are rising. I have read that in October 2022, conventional mortgage rates

rose above 7% for the first time in 20 years, and rates are expected to continue climbing as long as the Federal Reserve continues raising rates.

If your borrowers can't qualify for a conventional mortgage. Say they may have bad credit or a short credit history. They may have damaged their credit. They may not qualify for a conventional mortgage or the cost could be extremely expensive. Your family loan borrowers don't have to worry about credit checks or other financial scrutiny. It may be advisable, if you're issuing family home loans to do some due diligence, however, especially if you're counting on loan payments as part of your regular cash flow.

If your borrowers need to build credit you should note that payments on family housing loans will not appear on their credit reports or benefit their credit scores the way on-time payments on a conventional mortgage would. If wishes to sidestep estate taxes. Intra-family loans are popular tools for transferring wealth between generations in a way that avoids hefty estate taxes. One way this can work is for the family member(s) issuing the loan to give the borrower a tax-free gift each year, which the borrower then applies toward loan payments. If this strategy makes sense for your situation, keep in mind that the maximum allowable tax-free gift amount can change annually, and if that amount is insufficient to cover a full year's worth of payments, the borrower will have to pay the difference to keep the loan in good standing.

Conclusion

Intra-family loans can provide a great opportunity for borrowers to save money and afford homes they couldn't finance through other means. They also can be a great tool for parents and grandparents seeking to transfer wealth to their children or grandchildren while avoiding estate taxes that would apply to traditional property bequests.

Warning
Because there are significant legal and tax considerations around intra-family housing loans, it's highly advisable to consult an attorney or tax expert familiar with these matters to help ensure your loan is structured and documented in a way that will withstand

IRS scrutiny—and that both parties to the loan report payment and interest information correctly on their federal tax returns.

If you made it this far, congratulations..... You are on your way to build wealth. Please read this book again and again if need be, until the values in this book become your mindset and Your way of life.

Bonus
13 month Bankers Rule Planner / Example of a
Promissory Note
Interact with me on YouTube
https://youtube.com/@bankersrules

Example

Assets and Liabilities

Liabilities	Assets	Private bank
Car $400	Car $400	Car $4000
Mortgage $850	Mortgage $850	Mortgage $306,000
Boat $600	Boat $600	Boat $36,000
Credit Card $500	Credit Card $500	Credit Card $5,000
Phone $50	Phone $53	Total $351,000
Utilities/ living Expenses $2,000	Total $2,403	
Total $4,4400		

Bankers Rule Planner

MONTH OF:

INCOME

Date	Source	Amount

Assets

Date	Deposit	Paid Date	Balance

SAVINGS

Date	Deposit	Paid Date	Balance

MONTHLY

Total Income	
Total Budget	
Total Savings	
Total Expenses	

Liabilities

Bill	Amount	Due Date	Paid Date

Notes

Bankers Rule Planner

MONTH OF:

INCOME

Date	Source	Amount

SAVINGS

Date	Deposit	Paid Date	Balance

MONTHLY

Total Income	
Total Budget	
Total Savings	
Total Expenses	

Notes

Assets

Date	Deposit	Paid Date	Balance

Liabilities

Bill	Amount	Due Date	Paid Date

Bankers Rule Planner

MONTH OF:

INCOME

Date	Source	Amount

Assets

Date	Deposit	Paid Date	Balance

SAVINGS

Date	Deposit	Paid Date	Balance

MONTHLY

Total Income	
Total Budget	
Total Savings	
Total Expenses	

Notes

Liabilities

Bill	Amount	Due Date	Paid Date

Bankers Rule Planner

MONTH OF:

INCOME

Date	Source	Amount

Assets

Date	Deposit	Paid Date	Balance

SAVINGS

Date	Deposit	Paid Date	Balance

MONTHLY

Total Income	
Total Budget	
Total Savings	
Total Expenses	

Notes

Liabilities

Bill	Amount	Due Date	Paid Date

Bankers Rule Planner

MONTH OF:

INCOME

Date	Source	Amount

Assets

Date	Deposit	Paid Date	Balance

SAVINGS

Date	Deposit	Paid Date	Balance

MONTHLY

Total Income	
Total Budget	
Total Savings	
Total Expenses	

Liabilities

Bill	Amount	Due Date	Paid Date

Notes

Bankers Rule Planner

MONTH OF:

INCOME

Date	Source	Amount

SAVINGS

Date	Deposit	Paid Date	Balance

MONTHLY

Total Income	
Total Budget	
Total Savings	
Total Expenses	

Notes

Assets

Date	Deposit	Paid Date	Balance

Liabilities

Bill	Amount	Due Date	Paid Date

Bankers Rule Planner

MONTH OF:

INCOME

Date	Source	Amount

Assets

Date	Deposit	Paid Date	Balance

SAVINGS

Date	Deposit	Paid Date	Balance

MONTHLY

Total Income	
Total Budget	
Total Savings	
Total Expenses	

Liabilities

Bill	Amount	Due Date	Paid Date

Notes

Bankers Rule Planner

MONTH OF:

INCOME

Date	Source	Amount

SAVINGS

Date	Deposit	Paid Date	Balance

MONTHLY

Total Income	
Total Budget	
Total Savings	
Total Expenses	

Notes

Assets

Date	Deposit	Paid Date	Balance

Liabilities

Bill	Amount	Due Date	Paid Date

Bankers Rule Planner

MONTH OF:

INCOME

Date	Source	Amount

SAVINGS

Date	Deposit	Paid Date	Balance

MONTHLY

Total Income	
Total Budget	
Total Savings	
Total Expenses	

Notes

Assets

Date	Deposit	Paid Date	Balance

Liabilities

Bill	Amount	Due Date	Paid Date

Bankers Rule Planner

MONTH OF:

INCOME

Date	Source	Amount

SAVINGS

Date	Deposit	Paid Date	Balance

MONTHLY

Total Income	
Total Budget	
Total Savings	
Total Expenses	

Notes

Assets

Date	Deposit	Paid Date	Balance

Liabilities

Bill	Amount	Due Date	Paid Date

Bankers Rule Planner

MONTH OF:

INCOME

Date	Source	Amount

SAVINGS

Date	Deposit	Paid Date	Balance

MONTHLY

Total Income	
Total Budget	
Total Savings	
Total Expenses	

Notes

Assets

Date	Deposit	Paid Date	Balance

Liabilities

Bill	Amount	Due Date	Paid Date

Bankers Rule Planner

MONTH OF:

INCOME

Date	Source	Amount

SAVINGS

Date	Deposit	Paid Date	Balance

MONTHLY

Total Income	
Total Budget	
Total Savings	
Total Expenses	

Notes

Assets

Date	Deposit	Paid Date	Balance

Liabilities

Bill	Amount	Due Date	Paid Date

Bankers Rule Planner

MONTH OF:

INCOME

Date	Source	Amount

SAVINGS

Date	Deposit	Paid Date	Balance

MONTHLY

Total Income	
Total Budget	
Total Savings	
Total Expenses	

Notes

Assets

Date	Deposit	Paid Date	Balance

Liabilities

Bill	Amount	Due Date	Paid Date

Bankers Rule Planner

MONTH OF:

INCOME

Date	Source	Amount

Assets

Date	Deposit	Paid Date	Balance

SAVINGS

Date	Deposit	Paid Date	Balance

MONTHLY

Total Income	
Total Budget	
Total Savings	
Total Expenses	

Notes

Liabilities

Bill	Amount	Due Date	Paid Date

Bankers Rule Planner

MONTH OF:

INCOME

Date	Source	Amount

Assets

Date	Deposit	Paid Date	Balance

SAVINGS

Date	Deposit	Paid Date	Balance

MONTHLY

Total Income	
Total Budget	
Total Savings	
Total Expenses	

Notes

Liabilities

Bill	Amount	Due Date	Paid Date

Example of a Promissory Note

Promissory Note

Simple Interest

Principal Loan amount   Loan start Date

$_____   Day_____ Month_____, 20_____

On or before Date ___/____/20____ the borrower promises to pay in full the principal of $_____.____ with simple interest, rate of _____ percent (_____ %) per year to the Lender Jeff Steinbrunner. Full amount of this Note, principal plus interest totaling $_____.____

Borrower agrees to pay the sum of $_____._____ on the _____ Day each month until date specified above, Hereinafter known as the "Due Date".

{Late Fee – There shall be a late payment fee of $10.00 if not paid on time within five days of due date.}

_____/_____/_____

Borrower (signature)   Date

_____

Borrower (print Name)

_____

_____

Borrower (Address)

Promissory Note

Simple Interest

Principal Loan amount   Loan start Date

$_____   Day_____ Month_____, 20_____

On or before Date ___/____/20____ the borrower promises to pay in full the principal of
$_____.____ with simple interest, rate of _____ percent (_____ %) per year to
the Lender Jeff Steinbrunner. Full amount of this Note, principal plus interest totaling
$_____.____

Borrower agrees to pay the sum of $_____._____ on the _____ Day each month
until date specified above, Hereinafter known as the "Due Date".

{Late Fee – There shall be a late payment fee of $10.00 if not paid on time within five days of
due date.}

_____/_____/_____

Borrower (signature)   Date

_____

Borrower (print Name)

_____

_____

Borrower (Address)